MELBOURNE

KATHRYN WALKER

WORLD ALMANAC® LIBRARY

Please visit our web site at: www.worldalmanaclibrary.com
For a free color catalog describing World Almanac® Library's list of high-quality books
and multimedia programs, call 1-800-848-2928 (USA) or 1-800-387-3178 (Canada).
World Almanac® Library's fax: (414) 332-3567.

Library of Congress Cataloging-in-Publication Data

Walker, Kathryn, 1957-
    Melbourne / by Kathryn Walker.
        p. cm. — (Great cities of the world)
    Includes bibliographical references and index.
    ISBN 0-8368-5052-1 (lib.bdg.)
    ISBN 0-8368-5212-5 (softcover)
    1. Melbourne (Vic.)—Juvenile literature. I. Title. II. Series.
    DU228.W35   2005
    994.5'1—dc22   2005045463

First published in 2006 by
World Almanac® Library
A Member of the WRC Media Family of Companies
330 West Olive Street, Suite 100
Milwaukee, WI 53212 USA

Produced by Discovery Books
Editors: Betsy Rasmussen and Kathryn Walker
Series designers: Laurie Shock, Keith Williams
Designer and page production: Rob Norridge
Photo researcher: Rachel Tisdale
Diagrams: Rob Norridge
Maps: Stefan Chabluk
World Almanac® Library editorial direction: Mark J. Sachner
World Almanac® Library editor: Gini Holland
World Almanac® Library art direction: Tammy West
World Almanac® Library graphic design: Scott M. Krall
World Almanac® Library production: Jessica Morris

Photo credits: Getty Images/AFP/William West: p. 39; Getty Images/Glen Allison, cover and title page;
Getty Images/Tim Graham, p. 42; Getty Images/Hulton Archive, pp. 8, 10, 12, 13; Getty Images/Hulton Archive/
Keystone: p. 16; Getty Images/Regis Martin: p. 38; Getty Images Sport/Clive Brunskill: p. 28; Photographers Direct/
Philip Game Photography/Barbara Game: p. 27; Still Pictures/AAP: pp. 23, 30, 32; Still Pictures/Gavin Blue: pp. 20, 37;
Still Pictures/Rennie Ellis: pp. 18, 35; Still Pictures/Carolyn Johns, pp. 11, 22, 40; Still Pictures/Tom Keating: p. 25;
Still Pictures/Philip Quirk, pp. 4, 24, 34. 41; Still Pictures/Tony Yeates, pp. 7, 14, 17, 33.

Cover: Church spires and skyscrapers mingle in this view of Melbourne's Central Business District, seen from
across the Yarra River. The Yarra flows through the center of the city.

Printed in Canada

1 2 3 4 5 6 7 8 9 09 08 07 06 05

Contents

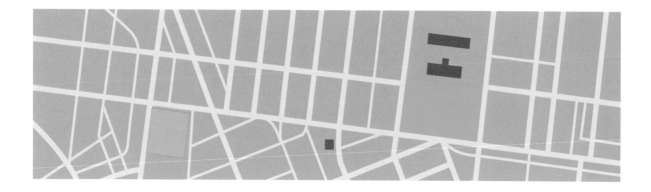

Introduction

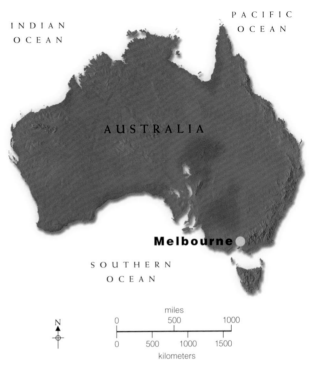

M elbourne is the capital of the Australian state of Victoria and home to almost three-fourths of Victoria's population. It is Australia's second-largest city after Sydney, and the rivalry between the two cities is legendary. Neither Melbourne nor Sydney is the national capital, however; that status belongs to Canberra, tactfully located halfway between the two.

Melbourne is sophisticated, cosmopolitan, and the most European of Australian cities in its style and architecture. It is famous for its

◄ Melbourne's city center is a mix of old and new. Here, the city's tallest building, Rialto Towers, soars above the Olderfleet Building in Collins Street.

sporting life, cutting-edge cultural scene, excellent dining, café culture, and its streetcars, which are called trams. While other Australian cities abandoned the use of trams years ago, they remain a vital and well-loved part of Melbourne's transportation system and a symbol of the city. Wide, tree-lined streets together with an abundance of public gardens and parks give the city a feeling of relaxed openness, while stately nineteenth-century buildings add a sense of solidity. Several surveys of international cities have rated Melbourne the "World's Most Liveable City."

Geography

Located on the southeast coast of Australia, Melbourne sits on a coastal plain at the northern end of Port Phillip Bay, around the mouth of the Yarra and Maribyrnong Rivers. The metropolitan area encompasses the city center together with a large suburban sprawl that has expanded mainly southward along the bay side and eastward to the Dandenong Ranges. The Yarra River—sometimes called

"Melbourne is a chameleon city where the world's continents come together in a blend of understated charm. She is magnificent yet welcoming, and the most jaded traveler will fall in love with her as they realize that a foreign city can feel like home."

—*Conde Nast Traveler* magazine

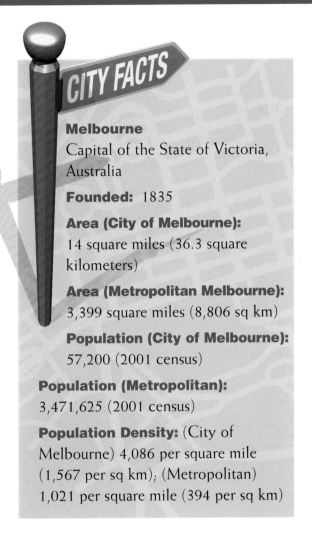

CITY FACTS

Melbourne
Capital of the State of Victoria, Australia

Founded: 1835

Area (City of Melbourne):
14 square miles (36.3 square kilometers)

Area (Metropolitan Melbourne):
3,399 square miles (8,806 sq km)

Population (City of Melbourne):
57,200 (2001 census)

Population (Metropolitan):
3,471,625 (2001 census)

Population Density: (City of Melbourne) 4,086 per square mile (1,567 per sq km); (Metropolitan) 1,021 per square mile (394 per sq km)

the "upside down river" because the mud seems to be on top—flows through the city, dividing it into north and south. The area known as the City of Melbourne is a municipality—a unit of government—that includes the Central Business District (CBD) and some historic inner suburbs.

City Layout

The heart of the city is a rectangular grid of streets that was laid out in 1837 on the north bank of the Yarra. This grid forms the CBD and covers an area of approximately

Metropolitan Melbourne

Melbourne City Center

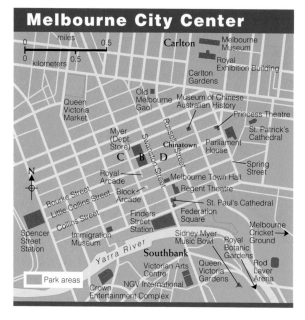

Victorian-era buildings that sit comfortably next to soaring skyscrapers. East of Swanston Street, Parliament House, Melbourne Town Hall, and the gothic spires of St. Paul's and St. Patrick's Cathedrals reflect the self-importance and wealth of nineteenth-century Melbourne.

Breaking the Grid

For many years, railroad lines formed a barrier between the city center and the Yarra River, but the opening of Federation Square (*see box, page 7*) in 2002 changed that. This big new development straddles the railroad artery, and, in doing so, it has freed the city center from the confines of its grid, extending it to the riverside. This change, together with other new developments across the river in the Southbank district, has shifted the city's center toward the Yarra.

Colorful Suburbs

Melbourne's suburbs have distinctive characters, and much of the city's charm lies in these neighborhoods. Just north of the CBD, the suburb of Carlton buzzes with bookstores, cafés, and university students. It is home to the Melbourne Zoo, the Melbourne Museum, and the splendid Royal Exhibition Building—the first Australian building to have been awarded World Heritage status. A more alternative and artistic edge exists near Fitzroy, where people of all backgrounds congregate at the bars and quirky stores of Brunswick Street. Moving southeast, South Yarra is a well-heeled, chic, and trendy

1 square mile (2.6 sq km). Its principal street running north to south is Swanston Street, while the main streets running east to west are Collins and Bourke. Lanes and alleyways, packed with cafés and stores, thread their way between the gridlines. The CBD contains some of the city's finest

Federation Square

Federation Square (pictured above) *opened in 2002, behind schedule, over budget, and different from its original plan. Despite all this, it seems as if the Square has succeeded in providing Melbourne with the central public meeting place it lacked. The 9-acre (3.8-hectare) site straddles twelve railroad lines, and it is built on a concrete and steel deck that incorporates spring coils and rubber pads to absorb vibrations from the trains. It contains a public plaza, a glass atrium, and a variety of buildings, all different from one another but each strikingly modern. They include the National Gallery of Victoria's Ian Potter Centre; the Australian Centre for the Moving Image; and an array of stores and restaurants.*

district that merges into the fashionable but less expensive suburb of Prahran. Farther south, the beachside suburb of St. Kilda has a busy esplanade, a pier, a historic amusement park, and a relaxed atmosphere.

Climate

Melbourne has four distinct seasons and, in general, a comfortable climate. Summer lasts from December through February, while the winter months are June through August. Summers are warm to hot with temperatures ranging on average between 58° Fahrenheit (14° Celsius) and 78° F (26° C) during February, typically the hottest month. It can get sizzling hot, however, with temperatures sometimes climbing to more than 104° F (40° C). The coldest month is July, when temperatures average between 42° F (6° C) and 56° F (13° C). Occasionally, there may be night frosts, but the city doesn't get snow. Spring is usually the wettest season.

Melbourne is known as a place where you can experience all four seasons in one day: Summer days can see sudden downpours and dramatic drops in temperature, while winter days can see warm sunshine. The local saying goes, "If you don't like the weather in Melbourne, just wait ten minutes."

CHAPTER 1

History of Melbourne

About fifty thousand years ago, maybe longer, the first settlers arrived on the landmass that is now Australia. It is generally believed that these ancestors of the first Australians, known as Aborigines, came across the ocean from Southeast Asia. At the time of the white settlements in the nineteenth century, the Aborigines that occupied the Victoria region were collectively referred to as the Koori. The Melbourne area was occupied by five Koori tribes that together formed the Kulin nation. The Kulin shared a common language, belief system, and culture that bonded them closely to the land. They lived by fishing, hunting, and gathering. Later, European settlers separated Aborigines from their land, which proved disastrous for this ancient culture.

White Settlers

Throughout the seventeenth and eighteenth centuries, the Australian coast was explored and mapped by Europeans. In 1770, Captain James Cook sailed along the eastern coast and claimed the land for Great

◄ *This picture shows Melbourne in about 1850; later in the same decade, the wealth of the gold rush years transformed the city with many stately buildings.*

Britain, naming this new addition to the British Empire New South Wales. At that time, the British government needed someplace to send its convicted criminals from the overcrowded prisons at home. So in 1788, the first ships carrying convicts and soldiers arrived at Botany Bay near Sydney, marking the beginning of the colonization of Australia.

The first European attempt at settling in the Melbourne area came in 1803, when Captain David Collins arrived with a group of settlers in an area near Sorrento on the Mornington Peninsula. Because of the lack of freshwater, however, they abandoned the settlement in 1804 and moved on. In 1834, Edward Henty, a farmer, left the convict colony on what is now the island state of Tasmania, at the southern tip of Australia, and established the first permanent white settlement in Victoria.

Foundation of Melbourne

In 1835, a party led by an entrepreneur named John Batman sailed up to Port Phillip Bay. He explored the area on behalf of an association of Tasmanians who wanted to establish themselves in that region. He met with local Kulins, and Batman claimed that during the meeting he bought, by treaty, 600,000 acres (243,000 hectares) of land, which he paid for with blankets, tomahawks, knives, scissors, mirrors, handkerchiefs, flour, shirts, and an annual rent to be paid. It is possible that the Aborigines believed they were being paid for the right to pass through

Two Founders

To this day, people dispute who founded Melbourne. Batman died young in 1839, but Fawkner lived well into his seventies and made it his business to be deeply involved in many aspects of the new town's development by "poking his nose into every public movement," as one writer of the time said. Batman remains a controversial figure. Doubt remains about the genuineness of his treaty with the Aborigines, and most agree the price he paid for the land was low. Some say, however, that his treaty at least acknowledged the Aborigines' right to the land. It took more than 150 years for any Australian government to officially do that.

". . . I am glad to state about six miles up, found the river all good water and deep. This will be the place for a village."

—From John Batman's journal, 1835

their land; it's been said that the lives of the Aborigines were so closely linked to the land that it seems unlikely they would have knowingly sold it.

Associates quickly followed Batman, but, also in 1835, a rival party of settlers from Tasmania, organized by John Fawkner, arrived in the area. After some dispute, both the Batman and Fawkner parties settled down, but the governor of New South Wales, Sir Richard Bourke, proclaimed that, as the area was part of New South Wales, all settlers were trespassing on British Crown land. In the eyes of the government, it had not been the Aborigines' land to sell.

In reality, though, Governor Bourke, so far away in Sydney, could do little about the situation, and in 1837 he sent Captain William Lonsdale to administer the rapidly expanding settlement, then numbering about two hundred. A variety of place names for the area were considered, including Beargrass and Batmania. Luckily for today's Melburnians, neither of those names stuck; the settlement officially became Melbourne in 1837, named for the British prime minister, Lord Melbourne (1834–1841).

When Sir Richard Bourke visited the Port Phillip settlement in 1837, Robert Hoddle, a surveyor who eventually drew up plans for the city, accompanied him. His symmetrical grid of wide streets still forms the heart of Melbourne. In 1847, Melbourne officially became a city. It remained, however, part of

New South Wales—something Melbourne's citizens deeply resented. Melbourne's desire for separation was fulfilled when, in 1851, Queen Victoria of Great Britain declared the Port Phillip area to be the colony of Victoria, officially separate from New South Wales.

The Dispossessed

While European settlers poured into Victoria, the number of Aborigines there dropped from about fifteen thousand in 1834 to less than two thousand by 1860. There were several reasons for this dramatic decline. Some died in conflict with the settlers; many died of European-borne diseases such as smallpox and influenza; others were massacred or poisoned by the white settlers. Above all, the Aborigines were dying because they were dispossessed. They had lived in a delicate and sustainable balance with the land; the land was inseparable from their beliefs, their traditions, and their way of life. Without it, they were lost.

Settlers widely regarded the Aborigines as less than human. Concerned for the Aborigines' welfare, the British government

▼ *This picture shows what Melbourne looked like in 1838, the time when it was still a small settlement on the banks of the Yarra River.*

▲ *Sovereign Hill at Ballarat, west of Melbourne, is a re-creation of an 1850s gold mining town. It was in this decade that the discovery of gold at Ballarat sparked one of the world's biggest gold rushes.*

set up a protectorate system in 1835, with appointed "protectors" to look after and represent the Aboriginal population. The system did not work, however, and the government abandoned it in 1849. In 1860, the British government set up the Central Board for the Aborigines. It adopted a policy of establishing reserves and mission stations where the natives could live under the control of the Central Board.

Gold Fever

In 1851, shortly after Victoria became a separate colony, Melbourne was turned upside down by the discovery of gold in Ballarat, about 68 miles (110 km) northwest of the city. Shiploads of migrants from around the world flooded into Melbourne

"The whole town of Geelong is in hysterics, gentlemen foaming at the mouth, ladies fainting, children throwing somersets [somersaults] with excitement. All the ruffians and rogues from Melbourne and the scum of convicts from Van Dieman's Land moved in a surge towards Ballarat."

—*Melbourne Argus*, describing the Gold Rush in Victoria, September 21, 1851

on their way to the goldfields, where they hoped to make their fortunes. At that time, Melbourne was not a pleasant place to live; the city was muddy, dirty, violent, and downright smelly. It was not equipped to cope with this massive influx of people. Cities of canvas tents sprung up along the banks of the Yarra to house newcomers, while filth piled up in the streets. The city's workers, including the police, deserted their regular jobs to join the hunt for gold. With so few left to run the city, chaos reigned in those first years of the gold rush.

Marvelous Melbourne

Soon, Victoria was producing more than one-third of the world's gold. The great

wealth this brought transformed the city and was reflected in beautiful public buildings and extravagant mansions. The 1860s heralded a period of great prosperity and progress for Melbourne, and it overtook Sydney as Australia's financial center. By 1861, Melbourne's population of 125,000, made it the largest city in Australia.

During the 1880s, Melbourne's extravagance seemed to reach fever pitch with increasingly elaborate building projects undertaken. Visitors called it the "Paris of the Antipodes" and "Marvelous

▼ *This photograph of Collins Street in Melbourne's business district was taken in about 1875. Elegant buildings reflect the city's prosperity at this time.*

▲ *Many people regard Victorian outlaw Ned Kelly (1834–1880) as a great folk hero. He is pictured here in a shoot-out wearing the famous bucketlike helmet that was part of his homemade armor.*

Old Melbourne Gaol

Located on Russell Street in the CBD, the gloomy Old Melbourne Gaol (prison) is now a museum, and it is a popular, if somewhat gruesome, attraction. The main reason for its popularity is Ned Kelly, the gaol's most famous prisoner, who has been immortalized in ballads, books, and movies. Kelly and his gang were notorious Australian outlaws, and by the time Kelly was finally caught and executed in 1880, his stand against authority had made him a hero in the eyes of many, while others maintained he was a murderous villain. Kelly and his family had a troubled relationship with the Victoria police, whom he colorfully described as "ugly fat-necked wombat headed big bellied magpie legged narrow hipped splaw-footed sons of Irish Bailiffs or English landlords," in a long letter he dictated in 1879, known as the Jerilderie letter. The letter is currently kept at the State Library of Victoria along with Kelly's weird-looking suit of homemade armor. Visitors to the gaol can see the gallows where Kelly and other prisoners were hanged, along with displays of the prison's most colorful inmates and some death masks, including that of Ned Kelly.

Melbourne." The city had electricity, trams, and a telephone system. The suburbs began to spread, and buildings at the heart of the city moved upward, lace-like ironwork embellished its fine houses, and land prices boomed. Until the city's sewage system was properly set up in 1891, however, some also knew it as "Marvelous Smellbourne."

End of the Golden Era

The bubble burst, however, and the boom years ended along with the 1880s. In Melbourne, houses and land had become overpriced and the property market finally collapsed. Events in overseas financial

markets caused foreign investment in Australia to dry up. A severe economic depression affected the country's eastern states. In Melbourne, banks and other businesses shut down and people lost their jobs and fortunes.

Federation

In 1901, Australia's six colonies united to form the nation of Australia. Melbourne, by then recovered from its depression, became, for a time, the Australian capital and the seat of the national government. (In 1927, the newly built city of Canberra became the capital.) Great celebrations took place when the Duke and Duchess of Cornwall, the future King George V and Queen Mary

▲ *Built for the 1880 International Exhibition, the Royal Exhibition Building was the venue for the ceremonial opening of the first Federal Parliament in 1901.*

of Great Britain, came to Melbourne to open the first Federal Parliament. Melbourne entered another period of growth and development.

The Great Depression

Things once more came skidding to a halt when the global Depression of the 1930s hit Australia, bringing unemployment and poverty. To help provide jobs, the government launched a series of public works, such as the Great Ocean Road, the Yarra Boulevard, St. Kilda Road, and the

Shrine of Remembrance—a memorial to those who died in World War I. Unemployed men did the backbreaking work on these projects for which they received a small amount of money.

A Loosening of Bonds

During World War II (1939–1945), Australia entered the war on the side of the Allies and fought alongside the British in Europe. After the Japanese bombed Pearl Harbor in 1941, Australia faced the very real threat of invasion by Japan. It was, however, not Great Britain but the United States that helped Australia fight off the enemy. General Douglas MacArthur arrived in Melbourne in 1942 and set up the Pacific War Headquarters on Collins Street, and the Melbourne Cricket Ground temporarily became a U.S. Air Force base.

Lack of support from Britain during the war marked the loosening of the old bonds between the two countries. Australia's loyalties shifted away from the United Kingdom and toward the United States; trade with Britain declined, and, in the

"Without any inhibitions of any kind I make it quite clear that Australia looks to America, free of any pangs as to our traditional links or kinship with the United Kingdom."

—John Curtin, Australian prime minister, the *Melbourne Herald*, December 1941.

Saying Sorry

In Victoria, as in other Australian states, authorities had the right to forcibly remove the children of Aborigines from their homes in order to break their ties with their own culture and integrate them into white Australian society. The authorities used these powers extensively from 1910 onward, and the brutal practice of splitting up families was still going on as recently as 1970. In 1997, an inquiry looked into these enforced separations. Its report was shocking in its account of the pain, suffering, and abuse caused to those children and their families. On May 26 of each year, in what is known as Sorry Day, many communities across the country get together to acknowledge the many injustices heaped upon Australia's original inhabitants, in an attempt to help the process of healing and reconciliation. As of 2005, Prime Minister John Howard expressed regret, but would not apologize on behalf of the nation because he felt that no one should be held responsible for what happened in the past.

decades that followed, Australia began to build trade links closer to home, within the Pacific Rim region. The vulnerability that Australia felt during wartime was one of the reasons it launched a huge immigration campaign after the war. Australia felt it needed a larger population in order to defend itself in times of danger—"populate or perish" was the slogan of the time. Also, it needed more people to boost its workforce

"The Friendly Games"

The lead-up to the 1956 Olympic Games was anything but promising. There were arguments within Australia about the financing of the Games, and preparations fell behind schedule badly. Melbourne got back on track, but world events caused more problems. Shortly before the Games opened, the Soviet Union invaded Hungary, causing the Netherlands, Spain, and Switzerland to withdraw in protest; Egypt, Iraq, and Lebanon withdrew because Britain and France had invaded Egypt; and the People's Republic of China withdrew because the Republic of China (Taiwan) had been allowed to take part in the Games. This backdrop was not exactly "friendly," but relations between the competitors were, on the whole, excellent. The only problem was the infamous water polo match between Hungary and the Soviet Union, remembered as the "Blood in the Water Game," which turned, quite literally, into a bloodbath, as the competitors fought one another to the point of injury. Australia won thirteen gold medals that year. The picture (above) shows the opening ceremony at the main stadium.

and economy. This new surge of immigration brought people to Melbourne from a variety of European countries and breathed new life into the city.

Postwar Melbourne

The postwar years saw rapid growth in Melbourne's industry and population. In the CBD, the noise of construction work and the dust of demolition filled the air, while new housing in the suburbs caused the city to spread farther across the landscape. Melbourne got the chance to shake off its stuffy colonial image and present a new face to the world when, against the odds, the International Olympic Committee chose it to host the 1956 Olympic Games. Despite a stormy political backdrop (*see box*), the Olympics were a great success, and Melbourne proved itself an excellent host.

Since 1916, buildings in Melbourne had been limited to a height of 130 feet (40 meters)—the height to which firefighters' ladders could reach. In 1957, Melbourne abandoned this limit, and the first skyscraper broke through the skyline in 1958, followed shortly by many others. During the 1960s and 1970s, developers tore down large areas of Victorian-era housing in the city center and inner suburbs to make way for new developments.

More Boom and Bust

The 1980s were a boom time, with property prices climbing higher and higher. In 1990, however, Australia's property market came

▲ *The huge Crown Entertainment Center and Casino in the city's Southbank district opened in 1997 and contains Australia's largest casino.*

crashing down, resulting in an economic recession and unemployment that hit Melbourne hard. The Labor Party had governed Victoria since 1982, but, in 1992 and again in 1996, Victorians voted for a new style of government with the Liberal-National Coalition, headed by Jeff Kennett. Kennett's tough, brash, and single-minded style inspired strong feelings: He was either loathed or loved. His solution to Victoria's economic crisis was to sell off publicly owned services and cut public spending. He embarked on several major, often controversial, projects. These included putting a Grand Prix racetrack into Albert Park, and developing Federation Square and the Crown Entertainment Centre and Casino. During his time, the economy recovered, but sectors such as health, education, and welfare suffered. He lost the 1999 election to the Labor Party with Steve Bracks as its leader.

At present, big construction projects continue to progress, and the redevelopment of Melbourne's Docklands is the largest project of its kind in the country. It involves developing an area about the same size as the CBD that will include offices, residential areas, entertainment and sport facilities, shops, and restaurants. It is part of a program of development that is radically enlarging Melbourne's city center and extending it down to the waterfront.

CHAPTER 2

People of Melbourne

The nearly 3.5 million people who live in metropolitan Melbourne come from many different ethnic backgrounds. According to the 2001 census, almost 30 percent of the population was born in countries other than Australia. Because the first white settlers to Australia were mainly from Britain, the national language is English. More recently, however, immigration from many other countries has increased. As a result, at least one-fourth of today's Melburnians speak a language other than English at home. The census also showed that in 2001, twelve thousand indigenous people were living in Melbourne, representing just 0.4 percent of the population.

Waves of Immigration

In the 1850s, the discovery of gold in Victoria brought a huge influx of people from around the world, all hoping to make their fortunes. The majority were British and Irish, but there were also large numbers of Chinese, Germans, and Americans, as well as smaller numbers of people from other countries. Another major surge of

◀ *Melbourne has a vibrant café life and excellent restaurants. This café-bar is part of a well-known restaurant in the popular bay side suburb of St. Kilda.*

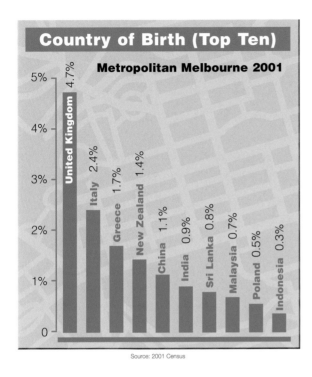

Country of Birth (Top Ten)

Metropolitan Melbourne 2001

- United Kingdom 4.7%
- Italy 2.4%
- Greece 1.7%
- New Zealand 1.4%
- China 1.1%
- India 0.9%
- Sri Lanka 0.8%
- Malaysia 0.7%
- Poland 0.5%
- Indonesia 0.3%

Source: 2001 Census

◀ *The 2001 census showed that almost 30 percent of the population of metropolitan Melbourne was born overseas. This chart shows the percentages of the population born in the top ten overseas countries.*

immigration came after World War II, as Jewish survivors of the Holocaust and others escaping postwar hardship came to Melbourne to make new lives for themselves. Greeks, Turks, Maltese, Italians, and Yugoslavians were part of this influx. Significant numbers of Southeast Asian immigrants began to arrive in the 1970s, often as refugees from war-torn Vietnam and Cambodia, while the 1980s brought immigrants from Africa.

"White Australia Policy"

During the gold rush years, white Australians, particularly miners, strongly resented the large numbers of Chinese newcomers. On the goldfields, the Chinese were tireless and careful workers, good at finding gold where others failed to find it.

This, together with the low wages for which the Chinese were willing to work, caused whites to view them as unwelcome competition. The Chinese became objects of suspicion and abuse. When the new federal parliament formed in 1901, it quickly passed a law preventing all non-European immigration. After World War II, increasing public dislike of this unfairness and of racial discrimination led the government to gradually relax these restrictions and to dismantle the infamous "White Australia Policy" in the 1970s.

Immigration Today

Australia now operates a "nondiscriminatory" immigration program—people cannot be refused entry because of where they were born or their ethnic origin. Instead, they are judged on their language abilities, skills, and ages. Close relatives of people already living in the country or those whom the authorities believe need refuge from civil war or human rights abuses are allowed in. The number of immigrants is now tightly controlled, and many applicants are refused entry.

Multicultural Melbourne

Various parts of Melbourne have become associated with particular cultural groups. The oldest of these precincts is Chinatown

▲ *The Chinese New Year celebrations, held in late January or early February, always draw big crowds to Melbourne's Chinatown, located in the CBD.*

in the CBD, based around Little Bourke Street. This area of nineteenth-century buildings and lanes was a center for the spurned Chinese community in the 1850s. Today, it bustles with Chinese restaurants, shops, and cafés. The Museum of Chinese Australian History at Cohen Place tells the history of Melbourne's Chinese community.

Melbourne's Greek community is the third largest in the world—only the Greek cities of Athens and Thessaloniki have larger Greek populations. The area around Lonsdale and Russell Streets in the CBD has many Greek shops, bars, and restaurants. The area often referred to as "Little Vietnam" centers on Richmond's Victoria Street, while, just north of the city, the suburb of Carlton has its "Little Italy" at Lygon Street.

A Jewish community has been in Melbourne since the 1840s. Today numbering about fifty thousand, it is the largest Jewish community in Australia. The southern suburb of St. Kilda and adjoining Caulfield is the area sometimes affectionately referred to as the "the bagel belt." St. Kilda is home to the Jewish Museum of Australia, and nearby Elsternwick is home to the Jewish Holocaust Museum and Research Centre. Acland and Carlisle Streets in St. Kilda are well known for their Jewish food stores, coffeehouses, and cake shops.

Religion

In the 2001 census, more than 70 percent of Melbourne's population said they held religious beliefs. The city has numerous churches, mosques, temples, Buddhist centers, and synagogues that provide for people of many religions.

Christianity in Melbourne

The first British settlers brought Christianity to Melbourne and all of Australia, both as Roman Catholicism and in various Protestant forms. According to

A Bond of Suffering

In Germany, November 1938 heralded the beginning of the organized violence and persecution against Jews under Adolf Hitler's Nazi regime. In December of that year, a group of Koori elders, led by William Cooper, arrived at the German Consulate in Melbourne to present the German government with a resolution condemning the persecution of German Jews. These Kooris were the first Australians to protest against the situation. Like the German Jews, they knew what it was like to be treated as less than human and to be denied citizenship of their own country. This special bond of understanding has led many Jewish people to be actively involved in campaigns for Aboriginal rights. Some of them are lawyers who have acted on behalf of the Aborigines. The Jewish Holocaust Museum and Research Centre now has a plaque commemorating the protest. At its unveiling, the president of the Centre said: "The world was silent—except here on this island continent of barely seven million people, a group, an ancient people, took action. We salute them."

the 2001 census, the majority of those Melburnians who held religious beliefs— about 63 percent—were Christians. Catholicism was the most widely followed of all the Christian denominations, followed by Anglicanism (a form of Protestantism that began in England). In Melbourne, however, churchgoing numbers are fairly low, as is the case elsewhere in Australia.

Melbourne's cathedrals are among its most notable landmarks. The triple-spired St. Patrick's Cathedral, on the eastern edge of the CBD, is a graceful Roman Catholic cathedral built in Gothic style that dates in part from 1857. The Anglican cathedral of St. Paul's is a majestic building dating from 1880, also in the Gothic style.

Some of Melbourne's Christian population follows the Eastern Orthodox forms of worship. Melbourne's Greek Orthodox community is one of the oldest in Australia, and its Evangelismos Church in East Melbourne, built in 1902, was Victoria's first Orthodox church.

Other Religions in Melbourne

The number of Hindus, Muslims, and Buddhists is growing in Melbourne. The 2001 census showed that Buddhism, with more than 3 percent of the population, had the biggest following of all the non-Christian religions; about 2.5 percent were Muslims; just over 1 percent were Jewish; and less than 1 percent were Hindus.

Festivals and Celebrations

Throughout the year, Melbourne's calendar bursts with events and festivals, some of which seem to take over the entire city. Most of these big festivals do not revolve around religion, although Christmas is widely celebrated with plenty of events around the city and, together with Easter, it is a public holiday. Many of Melbourne's ethnic communities hold festivals that

Barry Humphries

Born in Melbourne in 1934, comedian Barry Humphries began his career writing and performing sketches while a student at the University of Melbourne. Onstage, he has created a variety of comic Australian characters. They include a foul-mouthed and beer-drinking Australian cultural attaché and a purple-haired Melbourne "housewife-superstar" called Dame Edna Everage (pictured above with a koala), who is now probably the most famous of his characters. Edna has her own talk shows, which she describes as being "like an intimate conversation between two friends, one of whom is a lot more interesting than the other." Barry Humphries says that through his characters, he aims to encourage people to look at Australia critically but with affection and humor. He now lives in Britain and the United States. He is also a film producer, an award-winning author, and a highly successful artist.

celebrate their culture with traditional food, drink, and music. The Lygon Street Festa, held during October in "Little Italy," features a waiters' race, greasy pole climbing, and pizza throwing. In March or April, Lonsdale Street is the focus of the Antipodes Festival that celebrates Greek culture with everything from concerts and exhibitions to cake-eating competitions.

In September, the Royal Melbourne Show, held in the Royal Melbourne Showgrounds, gives city dwellers a taste of the country with rodeos, sheep shearing events, and a tomato fight. The Moomba Festival, one of Australia's largest outdoor events, is held in March. It crackles into life along the Yarra River for an action-packed few days. Fireworks light the sky, and many sporting events such as dragon-boat racing and water skiing occur. The highlight is the procession of floats that ends the festival.

Food Capital

Melbourne is undeniably one of the world's top cities for dining. The city's enthusiasm for the good things in life bubbles over in March at the Food and Wine Festival, a series of events that involve eating, cooking, and wine tasting.

Each ethnic area of the city has good restaurants, cafés, and stores that specialize in foods from particular countries. Italian food is generally very popular, as are light and spicy Thai and Vietnamese cuisines. Exposure to so many different cooking styles has helped create a uniquely

"They say one meal in four is eaten out, and you can see why. They [Melbourne's restaurants and bars] are cheap, serve fantastic food from a huge variety of influences and cultures and are widely patronized."

—Paul Bethell, journalist and lecturer, in *BBC News World Edition*, 2002.

Australian cuisine, known as Modern Australian or "Mod Oz." Mod Oz skilfully fuses elements of Asian, European, and Mediterranean cooking in dishes that are typically light, fresh, and tasty.

Bush Tucker

There is a revival of interest in cooking with the native Australian plants and animals that the Aborigines lived off for thousands of years. Some of Melbourne's top restaurants now feature dishes that use native foods, known as "bush tucker." Kangaroos, possums, crocodiles, witchetty grubs (wood-boring caterpillars), and baby eels are all kinds of bush tucker that might appear on the menu. Native fruits such as the *kakadu* plum (the richest source of vitamin C in the world), the *quandong* (a type of peach), and *riberry* fruits are often used for making sauces.

Beverages

Sometimes called the coffee capital, Melbourne is passionate about coffee and

▲ *A highlight of Melbourne's Food and Wine Festival is "The World's Longest Lunch," an event in which one thousand diners take their seats at a very long table.*

has a thriving café scene. According to the Melbourne newspaper, *The Age*, there are twelve thousand seats in the city center's outdoor cafes upon which to sit and drink coffee. The Yarra Valley northeast of Melbourne produces about 20 percent of Australia's wines. There is a strong tradition of beer drinking in Melbourne, as elsewhere in Australia, and many different brews are served in the many bars around the city.

CHAPTER 3

Living in Melbourne

Metropolitan Melbourne sprawls over 3,399 square miles (8,806 sq km). Its population is relatively thinly spread across that area, partly because this "Garden City" has a large proportion of green spaces and partly because of the large number of single-family houses in the suburbs.

Changing Patterns

After World War II, Melbourne's suburbs started to spread because of the rapidly increasing population. People wanted to move from the more crowded city center to larger houses, ideally with at least a one-quarter acre (0.1 hectare) lot. Melbourne became a "doughnut city" with almost everyone living around the center. Recently, however, many people are beginning to favor the buzz of the revitalized central areas over the open space and yards of the suburbs. The number of people living in the CBD has risen dramatically. Between 1996 and 2001, its population increased at a rate of 26 percent per year, and the number of dwellings there has almost doubled during that time.

◀ *The lace-like ironwork decorating this house in South Melbourne is a typical feature of many of the city's older dwellings.*

▲ Built in the early 1890s, the Block Arcade in the CBD houses cafés and a mixture of unusual and exclusive stores.

"Really we found very little wrong with Melbourne, it's just about the perfect city."'

—Bill Ridgers, member of the Economist Intelligence Unit's editorial staff, talking about the EIU's "World's Most Liveable City Survey" in *The Age*, October 2002.

Shopping

Along with eating out and drinking coffee, shopping is a favorite pastime among Melburnians. The heart of the city has large department stores, multilevel shopping malls, specialty shops, chic boutiques, and a bustling market, all within a reasonably compact area. The famous Myer department store, a Melbourne institution, sits on Lonsdale Street, covering almost two blocks and selling just about everything. Close by and a little more upscale is another major department store called David Jones.

Little Collins Street and Collins Street in the CBD are the places to go for top designer wear, while the upper end of Collins, or "Paris End," has the most exclusive jewelry, international designer stores, and high price tags. Woven between the main shopping streets are some historic alleys and shopping areas with smaller stores selling all kinds of unusual things. The charming Block Arcade in Collins Street is famous for its mosaic floors and murals, and the Royal Arcade on Little Collins Street is the oldest shopping mall in Australia. The CBD is a good place to buy opals, a specialty of Australia. It also has galleries and stores that sell indigenous artwork, now very much sought after and expensive.

Fashion and Bargain Trails

Good shopping is not confined to the city center, however, and Melbourne's large suburban shopping complexes have posed something of a threat to business in the CBD. Chadstone—The Fashion Capital, for example, is a huge and popular complex located south of the city center with more than four hundred outlets. Also, some suburbs have their own high-profile shopping strips, such as South Yarra and Prahran. The trendy come here to shop, particularly around Chapel Street, where the stylish fashion stores and sidewalk cafés are considered to be the coolest places to be seen. Richmond is renowned for its factory outlets where you can buy designer-label "seconds" at greatly reduced prices.

Markets

Some fun and interesting markets around the city include Prahran Market, well known for its excellent delicatessens, and St. Kilda Arts and Crafts Market. The largest and most famous is the Queen Victoria Market located just north of the CBD. Dating from the nineteenth century, it covers a vast 15 acres (6 hectares) and has hundreds of indoor and outdoor stalls. Fresh produce of all kinds goes on sale here, but so do clothing, souvenirs, craftwork, knick-knacks, and more. The color and bustle make it a big tourist draw, particularly in the summer when Wednesday's Gaslight Night offers everything from fashion shows to camel rides for entertainment.

Education

Children in Melbourne have to attend school from about age six to age fifteen. Public schools are usually co-educational and nonreligious. High school begins when students are twelve years old. They can leave after completing tenth grade, but the majority choose to stay on for the final two years. Most students who want to go to university then begin study for the Victorian Certificate of Education (VCE), a qualification based on assessment and examination in a chosen subject. Some schools, however, offer the International Baccalaureate instead—an internationally recognized qualification that makes it easier for students to gain places in certain overseas universities. Others opt to study for the Victorian Certificate of Applied Learning (VCAL), a vocational qualification that involves work-related experience.

Melbourne also has many private, or independent, schools, mainly associated with a particular religion. Private education is popular with some Melburnians, although the fees can be high. Some of these schools, such as Melbourne Grammar, Wesley College, and Scotch College, are famous throughout Australia.

Higher Education

Melbourne has seven major universities, including the prestigious University of Melbourne. Established in 1853, it is one of Australia's oldest universities and one of the world's best. The Royal Melbourne Institute

▲ *Students in a first grade class are pictured here making Christmas decorations at an elementary school in Brighton, a bay side suburb of Melbourne.*

of Technology (RMIT) is known for its strength in vocational and technical education. Monash University, the largest in the country and a leading research institute, attracts many overseas students. In addition, there are the TAFEs (Technical and Further Education institutions) that offer vocational training and diplomas or certificates. Some of the universities also run TAFE courses.

Traveling by Air and Sea

All international flights and the majority of domestic flights arrive at Melbourne Tullamarine Airport, about 14 miles (22 km) northwest of the city center. Transportation between the airport and the city center is not very good, however, with just one bus service operating the route. Cruise ships dock at Melbourne, but the only passenger services are to the nearby island state of Tasmania across the Bass Strait.

Road and Rail

Various companies run bus services connecting Melbourne with other state capitals. Two terminals for interstate and country buses operate: some from the Spencer Street Coach Terminal west of the city center, and others from the Melbourne Transit Centre, north of the city center. The train journey time from Melbourne to Sydney is between ten and eleven hours.

Getting around Melbourne

Trains are the most efficient way of getting to the outer Melbourne suburbs, and Flinders Street is the main suburban train station. Many trains running to or from Flinders pass through the City Loop, an

underground rail link that runs around the CBD. Melbourne has a public transportation network of trams, buses, and trains called Metlink, but it's usually referred to as "The Met." The city's much-loved trams provide extensive coverage of the city center and inner suburbs, while buses cover the parts not reached by trams.

The free City Circle tram service runs through the city center, stopping at places of particular interest. Taxis, always yellow, are plentiful and can be flagged down if their signs are lit. Another popular way of getting around is by bicycle. Because the Melbourne area is relatively flat, it is well

▲ A tram passes by the imposing Flinders Street Station. The building was completed in 1910, and its dome once contained a daycare center for children with access to a rooftop playground.

suited for cycling, and excellent biking trails wind throughout the city.

Driving in Melbourne
CityLink is a new automated tollway connecting three major arterials and allowing users easy and speedy access to the city. Users purchase an electronic CityLink pass or "E-Tag." (There are no tollbooths—the tags are automatically scanned.) The

"Meet Me under the Clocks"

Flinders Street Station is possibly Melbourne's most famous landmark and, like the trams, it has become a symbol of the city. This majestic red brick and cream stucco building sits at the intersection of Swanston and Flinders Streets, crowned with a stately dome. At the top of the steps to the main entrance is a row of clocks to show the departure times of the suburban trains, and "under the clocks" has been a favorite meeting place for generations of Melburnians. The station was completed in 1910, and it remains the busy hub of Melbourne's suburban railroad system.

system is proving highly controversial. Many people refuse to use CityLink because they object to paying the tolls.

Problems

Melbourne has a low crime rate that ranks it as one of the safest cities of its size in the world. Since 1998, however, there has been a string of gangland killings—believed to be connected to drug trafficking—that has resulted in more than twenty-five deaths. A problem with corruption within the Victoria police force also exists, particularly with regard to the drug squad. Many believe that this, combined with criticisms of the investigation into the gangland war, has shaken public confidence in the police force.

As is the case with many cities, Melbourne has issues such as drug addiction and homelessness. The 2001 census recorded more than fourteen thousand homeless people in Melbourne. A concern has grown over the increase in the number of people with gambling-related problems since electronic poker machines ("pokies") were introduced to Victoria in 1992. Many complain that the atmosphere of Melbourne's clubs and pubs has been destroyed by the presence of large numbers of these machines. Gambling has become a big source of revenue for the state government, however, which takes more than 15 percent in tax.

Environmental Issues

Some environmental problems exist as well. Because of water shortages, Melbourne now has restrictions on water usage, with stiff fines or even prison sentences for those caught breaking the laws. Although the water reservoirs are building up their supplies of water and people's water consumption in recent years has dropped, there is a need to continue in this way as the population grows and the predicted global climate change results in less rainfall. One of the causes of climate change is believed to be increasing greenhouse gas emissions. Victoria relies heavily on brown coal as a source of energy because there are huge reserves of brown coal in the nearby La Trobe Valley. Brown coal, however, is a very polluting form of energy, and Victoria is one of the biggest greenhouse gas polluters in the world. The government is now looking at ways to reduce its use of brown coal.

CHAPTER 4

Melbourne at Work

Victoria is Australia's most industrialized state; although it makes up just 3 percent of the landmass, it produces 26 percent of the nation's gross domestic product (the value of goods and services produced in a year). The state produces 57 percent of Australia's automotive production (vehicle production and the manufacture of parts). It is the biggest agricultural producer in the country and the largest exporter of food. Melbourne serves as Victoria's manufacturing center and international port. Melbourne is also a major financial services center—with businesses such as insurance, stock brokering, and investment banking—and about six hundred financial institutions have offices in the CBD.

An Attractive Location

Many multinational companies are choosing Melbourne as the place to base their Australian headquarters for a number of reasons. It costs less to set up business in Melbourne than it does in many other major cities; the city's high educational standards have created a particularly skilled and well-educated workforce; and there are speakers of many different languages among Melbourne's multicultural population

◀ Melbourne's seaport is the largest container and general cargo port in Australia; it handles 39 percent of Australia's container trade.

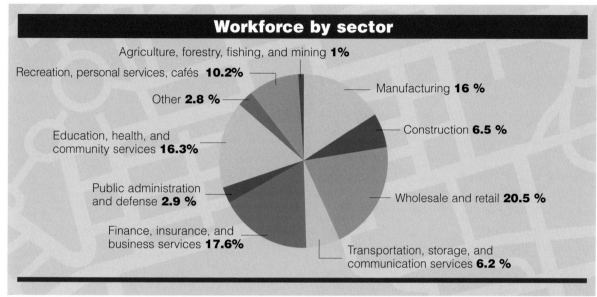

Workforce by sector

- Agriculture, forestry, fishing, and mining **1%**
- Recreation, personal services, cafés **10.2%**
- Other **2.8 %**
- Education, health, and community services **16.3%**
- Public administration and defense **2.9 %**
- Finance, insurance, and business services **17.6%**
- Manufacturing **16 %**
- Construction **6.5 %**
- Wholesale and retail **20.5 %**
- Transportation, storage, and communication services **6.2 %**

Source: Census 2001

whom multinational companies can employ. Furthermore, the city is a good location for serving markets within the Asia Pacific region, and the port facilities make it easy to export goods. Finally, the liveability of Melbourne itself, its good working conditions, and high standard of living make it an attractive location.

Biotechnology Capital

Melbourne is home to Australia's largest biotechnology industry, and it is a highly respected center for research in the field. Biotechnology involves the use of living material or biological processes to manufacture products or solve practical problems. It can be applied to agriculture, medicine, food science, and pharmaceutical production, as well as other areas.

Melbourne has made groundbreaking achievements in this field. They include

The Bionic Ear

In the late 1960s and the 1970s, a Melbourne University team led by Professor Graeme Clark worked on a device that would help profoundly deaf people to hear. Many thought this would be impossible, so no one would grant Graeme Clarke the money for his research. He was, however, determined to produce this device, known as a "bionic ear," or cochlear implant, so he tried hard to raise the money. Eventually, a television channel took up his cause and ran a telethon that brought donations flooding in. The generosity of people in Victoria combined with Graeme Clark's determination made it possible for the first person to receive the cochlear implant in 1978. The device involves a processor for converting sound into electrical impulses that are passed to the brain through twenty-two electrodes implanted in the inner ear. Today, more than fifty thousand people across the world can hear, thanks to the bionic ear.

"The Victorian Government is encouraging the development of a number of innovative research projects such as the synchrotron . . . . The goal is to work closely with industry to make Victoria one of the world's top 5 hubs for biotech science . . . ."—Invest Victoria, December 2004.

Monash University's research into in vitro fertilization (IVF)—a medical process used to help achieve pregnancy for those needing help—and the invention by a Melbourne University team of the "Bionic Ear" *(see box, page 31)*. To build on this strength, Victoria's government is currently

▼ *This picture shows what the city's synchrotron facility will look like when completed. The project will boost Melbourne's standing as a world leader in biotechnology and scientific research.*

constructing Australia's first synchrotron at Monash University. The synchrotron is a huge device that creates a form of light one million times brighter than sunlight. It helps scientists find out what molecules and matter look like. The information it gives them can be used for many purposes, such as creating vaccines, designing new drugs, and manufacturing microscopic machines.

Three Layers of Government

Australia is a federation of six states and two territories. Voting responsibilities are taken seriously. Throughout the country, people age eighteen and over can and must vote in both state and federal elections. Those that don't vote may face fines. Melbourne has three layers of government: the national, state, and local governments.

National and State Government

The top layer is the Government of Australia, or Commonwealth Government.

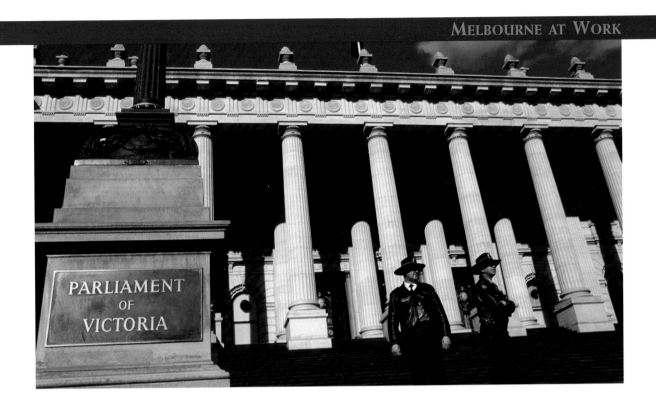

It controls the nation's foreign policy, defense, immigration, international trade, and the treasury. The national government is based in the Australian capital of Canberra.

Melbourne, as capital of Victoria, is home to the state government of Victoria. This second layer of government is made up of the Legislative Assembly and the Legislative Council. The Assembly consists of eighty-eight representatives elected to represent the different constituencies within Victoria, while the Council is made up of forty-four representatives elected from the state as a whole. The state government is responsible for planning major projects and for the provision of services such as policing, education, roads, and health care within Victoria. The head of the state government is the premier. Steve Bracks, leader of the Victorian branch of the Labor Party, was re-elected as premier in 2002.

▲ *The state government of Victoria meets at Parliament House, this large and impressive building located on Spring Street.*

Local Government

No single body represents the whole of Melbourne. Instead, the metropolitan area is divided into thirty-one municipalities, each with its own elected council. This system forms the third layer of government with each council responsible for local services such as garbage collection, planning, sanitation, and park maintenance. Councils also collect taxes from residents to pay for these services. A directly elected Lord Mayor heads Melbourne City Council, but the council does not represent the whole of metropolitan Melbourne. In this case, the "City of Melbourne" refers to the area that covers the CBD and some of the inner suburbs.

CHAPTER 5

Melbourne at Play

Melbourne is enthusiastic about sports. The city hosts some major international sporting events. One of the four tennis grand slam titles, the Australian Open, is held at the Rod Laver Arena. International cricket matches, both one-day matches and international "test" matches that can last up to five days, take place at the Melbourne Cricket Ground (MCG), and the Australian Formula One Grand Prix pulls in the crowds at Albert Park. The major horseracing event is the Melbourne Cup (*see box, page 35*), held at the Flemington Racecourse. It attracts international contestants and is watched on televisions around the world.

Aussie Rules

While cricket dominates the summer months, the most popular winter game is Australian Rules Football, also known as Aussie Rules, which has an almost religious following. This game originated in Melbourne in 1858, and although its popularity has spread throughout the country, the majority of teams in the Australian Football League are still from Melbourne. During the season, the newspapers are bursting with pages of Aussie Rules coverage, and its appeal to

◄ Crowds pack the Melbourne Cricket Ground for the Australian Football League Grand Final.

both sexes and all ages turns matches into family events. The season lasts through autumn and winter, culminating in the Grand Final at the end of September.

Other spectator sports include soccer, rugby, and basketball. Melbourne is closely associated with horse racing, and in October and November it is the setting of the Melbourne Spring Racing Carnival, the highlight of which is the Melbourne Cup.

"The Melbourne Cup is a brilliant and wonderful spectacle, a delirium of color, a vision of beauty. The champagne flows, everybody is vivacious, excited, happy; everybody bets, and gloves and fortunes change hands right along, all the time."

—Mark Twain, American author, 1895.

The Race That Stops a Nation

On the first Tuesday in November, Australia comes to a virtual standstill for the few minutes it takes to run the Melbourne Cup, the country's top horse race and a world-famous sporting event. In Melbourne, it is a public holiday. Champagne, fancy outfits, and big hats abound at the racecourse (pictured above) and a party atmosphere sparkles throughout the city. The best-loved Cup winner was the legendary New Zealand-born horse Phar Lap, who won in 1930 despite someone's attempts to shoot him on the day. In four years of racing, he won thirty-seven of the fifty-one races he entered. His sudden death at a California ranch in 1932 was never fully explained, and rumors of poisoning circulated. He had started life as a gangly and unlikely champion, and this, together with his gentle nature, made him an Australian hero.

The "G"

The game of cricket is somewhat similar to baseball and is played with a bat, ball, and eleven players on each team. The Melbourne Cricket Ground (MCG, often known simply as "the G") is Australia's most popular and revered sporting arena, with a seating capacity of approximately 100,000. One of the most famous cricket venues in the world, the MCG was the site of the first-ever international "test" match against England in 1877, which Australia won by forty-five runs. Strangely, Australia won the centenary test match held in 1977, by exactly the same number of runs. It is also home to the popular Australian Rules Football and is packed to capacity for the Grand Final that ends the season in September. The G was the focus of the 1956 Olympic Games, and today, sports memorabilia and interactive displays are housed in the MCG's Olympic Museum and Gallery of Sport.

Participation Sports

Outdoor activities include hiking and all kinds of water sports, such as canoeing on the Yarra River and rafting. The beaches offer swimming, sailing, and surfing. The Mornington and Bellarine Peninsulas are popular with surfers, but Bell's Beach near Torquay is the most famous surfing spot. The biggest open swim in the world is the Lorne's Pier to Pub, west of the city on the Great Ocean Road, when thousands take part in a three-quarter mile (1.2 km) swim from, as the name suggests, the pier to the pub.

Netball is very popular. This is a team game, similar to basketball, in which goals are scored by throwing a ball through a net at the top of a pole. Lots of people also play tennis, and public golf courses are located throughout the city, charging reasonable prices for a round of golf. Bike trails wind through and outside of the city. Resorts for cross-country and downhill skiing are spread out in the Victorian snowfields northeast of the city, some of them less than two hours' drive away.

City of Culture

Melburnians may be sports crazy, but this passion is matched by enthusiastic support for the arts. The city has many theaters, concert venues, art galleries, and museums. Added to this, it has a sparkling nightlife, with plenty of clubs and bars ranging from glamorous to grungy.

Some of the city's many festivals focus on a particular aspect of the arts, such as the International Comedy Festival, the Writers' Festival, or the Vibes on a Summer's Day music festival. Others are more wide-ranging, such as the Fringe Festival, which covers all things new and experimental in theater, art, and music, or the Melbourne International Festival of the Arts, a big event celebrating dance, music, opera, and theater.

Music and Theater

Many Australian rock bands have kicked off their careers by playing Melbourne's clubs and bars. These are still the places to hear

The Concert Hall is home to the Melbourne Symphony Orchestra, the Australian Ballet, and the Sydney-based Opera Australia; it also hosts concerts by a number of other visiting companies. Outdoor concerts, classical and nonclassical, are sometimes staged at the Sidney Myer Music Bowl, next to the Royal Botanic Gardens.

The city has an outstanding theater scene, both fringe and mainstream. The Melbourne Theatre Company (MTC) is Australia's oldest and most respected professional theater company. They stage their productions at the Victorian Arts Centre and at the Russell Street Theatre in the CBD. The Playbox Theatre is a company that stages new Australian plays at the CUB Malthouse complex in Southbank. In Carlton, an old factory houses the tiny La Mama Theater, a prized venue for experimental theater that has given many new playwrights their first break. The magnificent Princess Theatre in Spring Street and the stylish 1920s Regent in Collins Street provide more traditional settings; these cater more to the mainstream, and they often stage musicals.

Movies

Melbourne's long history of moviemaking began in 1906 when it produced Australia's first-ever (and possibly the world's first) feature-length movie, *The Story of the*

live music, not only rock and pop but also blues, jazz, and anything in between.

The riverside Victorian Arts Centre is the place to go for music of a more classical nature. The Centre incorporates the Melbourne Concert Hall and three theaters.

Archie Roach

Koori singer/songwriter Archie Roach (pictured above) *was born in an Aboriginal mission in Framlingham, Victoria, in 1956. Like thousands of Aboriginal children at that time, he was forcibly removed by the authorities from his family to be fostered by a series of white families—government policy at the time supported this practice in an attempt to integrate Aborigines into white society. He was about four years old when he was taken and was told that his family had died in a fire after he had left them. Years later, when he discovered the lie, he took to the streets with his guitar. In 1990, he released his first album that won various awards, including a Human Rights Award for his most well-known song* Took the Children Away, *in which he sings of the pain he shared with thousands of others. His powerful voice and haunting lyrics have earned him worldwide recognition.*

Kelly Gang. Melbourne continued to be an early pioneer in the field and still has its own movie industry that has produced some high-quality independent movies over the years. Each year, in late July and early August, the Melbourne International Film Festival screens hundreds of foreign films. There are also smaller festivals devoted to Italian and French movies. It isn't surprising, therefore, that while Melbourne has its share of large multiplex movie theaters offering the latest Hollywood releases, smaller venues show Australian, foreign, and independent movies.

Museums

In and around Melbourne are museums dedicated to a variety of subjects: shipping, sports, wool, surf, gold, the police, and even giant worms. The most wide-ranging is the Melbourne Museum, housed in a bold, modern building in Carlton Gardens, directly opposite and in stark contrast to the Royal Exhibition Building. It houses the award-winning Bunjilaka Aboriginal Centre, a major exhibition that explores and explains many aspects of the history and culture of Victoria's Aborigines. The Forest Gallery contains an indoor rain forest, while the Australia Gallery deals with the history and society of Australia, but with particular reference to Melbourne. Here you can see the noble racehorse, Phar Lap, now stuffed and in a glass case. Displays relating to him, and old newsreels, describe how a legend was born.

A central part of Melbourne's past and present is addressed in the excellent Immigration Museum, housed in the Old Customs House in the CBD. Recorded voices, letters, images, immigrants' belongings, and reconstructed ships' cabins help visitors understand the whole experience of immigration in terms of leaving home, journeying, and starting a new life.

Top Galleries

Melbourne has some excellent art galleries. Housed in a landmark steel building in the Southbank district, the Australian Centre for Contemporary Art (ACCA) is a major public art space devoted to temporary exhibitions. The National Gallery of Victoria (NGV) has recently split into two separate buildings, just a short stroll apart: the NGV International at St. Kilda Road and the Ian Potter Centre:

▲ *Charlotte Skene of the RMIT Gallery on Swanston Street adjusts a display of work by Aboriginal artist Joanne Currie Naligu that features beer bottles painted in traditional designs.*

NGV Australia at Federation Square—named for the businessman and philanthropist, Sir Ian Potter. NGV International, housed in a recently redeveloped 1960s building, has an impressive collection of international art and antiquities from many countries and eras. The new Ian Potter Centre in Federation Square houses a superb collection of Australian art, both indigenous and non-indigenous, from the nineteenth century to the present day.

Casino Culture

When, in the early 1990s, Melbourne got its first casino, there were many ruffled feathers

and squawks of outrage at bringing gambling to town. Like it or hate it, it's impossible to ignore the Crown Entertainment Centre and Casino sprawled along the banks of the Yarra River. This massive complex includes shops, clubs, movie theaters, and a hotel. It is glitzy and brash with a casino that has 350 gaming tables and more than 2,500 gaming and slot machines.

City Escapes

Melbourne has many outstanding parks and gardens that provide city dwellers with green spaces in which to relax. On the south bank of the Yarra River lies the magnificent Royal Botanic Gardens, one of the finest in the world. Just east of the CBD are the attractive Fitzroy Gardens, the unlikely location of Captain Cook's Cottage, which was transported from its original location in England in the 1930s. At the southern edge of the city, boats, canoes,

▲ The sunset parade of these Little Penguins at Phillip Island's Summerland Beach is one of Australia's most famous tourist attractions.

and yachts can be taken out on Albert Park Lake, while the nearby parks and beaches of the relaxed seaside suburb of St. Kilda make for a popular daytrip destination.

Sand and Sea

The coastline near Melbourne holds many attractions. To the east, the lovely beaches of the Mornington Peninsula have made the area a hit with vacationers and those looking for water sports. The Mornington Peninsula National Park has hiking trails and teems with wildlife. Just off the east side of the peninsula at Phillip Island is a koala conservation center, a brown seal colony at the aptly named Seal Rocks, and the home of the Little Penguins. Every evening at sunset, the Penguin Parade begins as these Little Penguins (also known as Fairy or Blue Penguins) come out of the sea and waddle home across the beach to nests in the dunes. On the western side of Port Phillip Bay, the Bellarine Peninsula has some popular seaside resorts.

The Great Ocean Road

Torquay is the start of one of the world's greatest coastal drives. The Great Ocean Road clings to the coastline, stretching about 174 miles (280 km) west to Warrnambool. Construction began on the road in 1919 and it is dedicated to the memory of those Australians killed in World War I. Some of the spectacular sights along the way include the famous offshore rock formation known as the Twelve Apostles, beaches and seaside towns, a rain forest, and the windswept Shipwreck Coast.

Inland Retreats

The Dandenong Ranges, about 20 miles (32 km) east of Melbourne, are home to forests and parks with plenty of wildlife and pretty villages. A great way to see the area is to take a ride on the Puffing Billy steam train that winds its way through the forests and fern gullies. Northeast of Melbourne, the major wine producing Yarra Valley attracts visitors with its natural beauty and tours of its many wineries. To the northwest, the Macedon Ranges offer mountain air, hiking, and amenities.

▼ *The Puffing Billy steam train carries sightseers over the Trestle Bridge at Sherbrooke Forest in the Dandenong Ranges.*

CHAPTER 6

Looking Forward

Experts predict that by 2030, the population of Melbourne will increase by roughly one million people. In 2002, the Victorian government, headed by Steve Bracks, published its plan for how best to cater to the housing needs of these extra people; the plan is called Melbourne 2030, and it has stirred up controversy.

Building for the Future

If the city continues to spread out around the edges to accommodate more people, the environmental costs will be high. Rural land will be lost, and there will be heavier reliance on private transportation, meaning more pollution. Melbourne is currently a low-density, sprawling city, and Melbourne 2030 intends to limit its outward spread by increasing housing within existing boundaries. The plan aims to encourage people to live around the fringes of Melbourne, to build on undeveloped city areas, and to concentrate expansion in more than one hundred "activity centers" throughout the city. An activity center is someplace where people work and live.

◄ *Australian model Elle MacPherson holds the baton at the launch of the Queen's Baton Relay in London on March 14, 2005. She is the first of thousands of runners who will carry the baton through all the Commonwealth nations to Melbourne for the opening ceremony of the 2006 Commonwealth Games.*

Many residents see a possible threat to the historic suburbs that are mainly low-rise nineteenth-century districts, and they want to protect the character and heritage architecture of their neighborhoods. Developers have already been coming forward with plans for large high-rise buildings for some of these areas.

Through rallies and other protests over some proposed high-rise developments, pressure groups have achieved some success. Steve Bracks announced in 2004 that, for the time being, metropolitan councils have the power to block developments over 30 feet (9 m) high in residential areas. Expanding Melbourne to accommodate the future population seems about to become a complicated balancing act.

The Commonwealth Games 2006

The Commonwealth of Nations is a voluntary association of self-governing states, most of which were once dependencies of Great Britain. Today, the purpose of the Commonwealth is largely to maintain friendly contact between the countries through cultural and sporting links, such as the Commonwealth Games. Melbourne has been chosen to host the eighteenth Commonwealth Games in 2006 and fully expects to repeat the success of the 1956 Olympics. In March 2006, top athletes from more than seventy nations will gather at Melbourne's MCG for the opening ceremony. Sixteen sports will feature in the Games.

"The 2006 Games are an extraordinary opportunity to generate investment in jobs and community infrastructure for Victoria's future. The benefits will be social, environmental, and economic— a legacy that will reaffirm Victoria as the place to be and Melbourne's reputation as the world's most liveable city."

—Justin Madden, Minister for the Commonwealth Games, 2004.

The Legacy

The Games Village is located just northwest of the CBD in the suburb of Parkville and will house the forty-five hundred athletes and officials. Designed to impress visitors, it is built with recycled products, featuring solar heating and water-recycling facilities. After the Games, it will provide new housing and parkland for the city, while facilities that have been upgraded or specially built for the occasion will benefit the public. The main responsibillity for organizing the Games lies with the Victorian Government. It hopes the Games will encourage tourism both during and after the event, while also helping forge new sporting and business relationships with other countries. Above all, the Games will give Melbourne the opportunity to show itself at its very best to the world.

Time Line

c. 50,000 B.C. The first Aborigines settle on the landmass that is now known as Australia.

A.D. 1770 Captain James Cook, the English navigator, anchors at Botany Bay and claims the land for Great Britain.

1788 The first ships carrying British convicts and soldiers arrive in Botany Bay.

1803 The first European attempt at settling in the Melbourne area is led by Captain David Collins but is abandoned in 1804.

1834 Edward Henty establishes Victoria's first permanent white settlement in Portland.

1835 John Batman sails to Port Phillip Bay; Batman makes a treaty with local Kulins to buy land for settlement. A party organized by John Fawkner also arrives in the area, and both groups settle in the Melbourne area.

1837 Captain William Lonsdale is sent by the governor of New South Wales to administer the new settlement. The settlement is officially named Melbourne. The surveyor Robert Hoddle draws up a grid plan for central Melbourne.

1847 Melbourne officially becomes a city.

1851 Queen Victoria declares the Port Phillip area to be the colony of Victoria, separate from New South Wales. Shortly afterward, gold is discovered close to Melbourne in Ballarat, sparking a gold rush and immigration to the city.

1861 With a population of 125,000, Melbourne becomes Australia's largest city.

1890s Melbourne and eastern Australia suffer a severe economic depression.

1901 Victoria becomes a state of the new Commonwealth of Australia. Melbourne becomes the Australian capital.

1927 Canberra becomes capital of Australia.

1930s The Great Depression brings hardship for many Australians.

1939–1945 Australians fight on the side of the Allies during World War II. Australia is threatened by attack from the Japanese. In 1942, U.S. General MacArthur arrives in Melbourne and sets up the Pacific War Headquarters.

1947 Thousands of immigrants from Europe begin to flood into Melbourne.

1956 Melbourne hosts the Olympic Games.

1970s The country abandons the "White Australia Policy," clearing the way for an influx of Asian immigrants.

1990 Economic recession hits Australia, and Melbourne suffers particularly badly.

1992–1999 Victoria elects a Liberal-National party coalition government with Jeff Kennett as premier.

1999 Victoria elects a Labor government headed by Steve Bracks.

2002 The Victorian government publishes the Melbourne 2030 plan.

2006 Melbourne hosts the eighteenth Commonwealth Games.

Glossary

Aborigine the original native inhabitants of Australia.

Antipodes the parts of the world directly opposite one's own country; often used to describe Australia and New Zealand.

arterials major streets or highways, often carrying large volumes of traffic.

biotechnology a technology based on the use of living organisms or biological processes, used in fields such as medicine, agriculture, pharmaceutical production, and food science.

colonization the process of a country acquiring and settling overseas territory.

Commonwealth a federation of states with powers divided between a central government and the governments of the individual states.

Commonwealth of Nations a voluntary association of more than fifty self-governing states, most of which were once dependencies of the United Kingdom; today, they remain linked by the desire to maintain friendly contact, mainly through cultural and sporting events.

container railroad-car sized shipping boxes that are loaded directly from ships to trains, by-passing the need to load and unload cargo by hand.

controversial causing controversy or disagreement.

death mask a plaster cast of a person's face, taken after that person has died.

droughts long periods of unusually low rainfall that result in water shortages.

esplanade a wide, flat walkway along the sea front.

gothic a style of architecture that is characterized by tall, pointed arches and spires.

Great Depression the period of financial hardship from 1929 to 1939, when people lost their jobs, homes, farms, and businesses.

Holocaust huge destruction and loss of life; capitalized, the term is often used to describe the mass killings of Jews by the Nazis during World War II.

immigration leaving one's native land and entering another country to make a new home there.

integration the act of making something open to people of all races.

Koori Aborigines of Eastern Australia.

Kulin Aborigine people of the five tribes or language groups that inhabited the Port Phillip region when the first European settlers arrived there.

mosaic a design made up of small squares of colored stone or glass.

municipality a district that has local self-government.

opals luminous gemstones that display bright flashes of color.

recession a period when a country's trade, economy, and employment is in decline.

suburban relating to the suburbs—districts that lie outside the city center.

test match an international cricket match that can last up to five days.

trams the name for streetcars in Australia and in the United Kingdom.

Further Information

Books

Banting, Erinn. *Australia: The Culture. Lands, Peoples, and Cultures* (series). Crabtree Publishing. 2002.

Bartlett, Anne. *Aboriginal Peoples of Australia. First Peoples* (series). Lerner Publishing, 2001.

Egger, Simone. *Lonely Planet: Melbourne.* Lonely Planet Publications, 2004.

Harrison, Tim. *Insight Guide: Melbourne.* Insight Guides, 2000.

Ritchie, Rod. *Fodor's Citypack: Melbourne.* Fodor's, 2001.

Sharp, Anne Wallace. *Australia. Indigenous Peoples of the World* (series). Lucent Books, 2002.

Townshend, Stephen. *The Rough Guide to Melbourne.* Rough Guides Ltd. 2002.

Web Sites

immigration.museum.vic.gov.au
The Immigration Museum site has an excellent time line that gives an account, decade by decade, of immigration to Victoria, as well as information on various aspects of immigration.

www.kooriweb.org/foley/index.html
Learn about Koori history through a time line, historical images, and newspaper articles.

www.melbourne.vic.gov.au/info.cfm
This City of Melbourne site gives lots of information on living in Melbourne.

www.museum.vic.gov.au
This Museum Victoria site has lots of information about Victorian wildlife as well as the history of the state.

www.sbs.com.au/gold/story.html
Find out about the impact the gold rushes had on Australia and what life was like on the goldfields through personal accounts on this lively site.

www.theage.com.au
Read articles from Melbourne's The Age *newspaper, covering a wide range of topics and views.*

Index

Page numbers in **bold** indicate pictures.